108 Messages

from your

Higher Self

Melanie Phillips

Published by Be The Light Publishing, September 2023

ISBN: 978-1-7753361-2-9

Copyright 2023 by Melanie Phillips

All rights reserved. No part of this publication may be reproduced, stored in or introduced into a retrieval system, or transmitted, in any form, or by any means (electronic, mechanical, photocopying, recording or otherwise) without the prior written permission of the publisher. This book is sold subject to the condition that it shall not, by way of trade or otherwise, be lent, resold, hired out, or otherwise circulated without the publisher's prior consent in any form of binding or cover other than that in which it is published and without a similar condition including this condition being imposed on the subsequent purchaser.

Editors: Eduardo Baldioceda and Marielle Soong
Book Cover Design: Sachia Kron

Readers of this publication agree that neither Melanie Phillips nor her publisher will be held responsible or liable for damages that may be alleged or resulting directly or indirectly from their use of this publication. All opinions in this book are those of the author.

For all who are here to create heaven on earth

Acknowledgements

I have so much love and gratitude to all who have supported me on my journey.

For some reason my family has never made me feel like I'm that much of a weirdo. Thank you Richard, Shirley and Lou, and Peter and Teresa for your unconditional love and support.

My heartfelt gratitude to my friends who have cheered me and this book on: Marielle Soong, Sachia Kron, Alison Denham, Mike Schauch, and Niki West.

I thank Source every day for bringing my partner, Eduardo Baldioceda Baltodano into my life. Thank you, Love, for your devotion, support and enthusiasm. You are the presence and the proof that life is a miraculous adventure.

Contents

Acknowledgements iv
Introduction vi
How to Use This Book vii
Why 108 Messages? viii
Daily Invocation and Intention ix
108 Messages 1

Introduction

Imagine living from a space inside yourself that is utterly aligned with the highest and best version of you ...

A vibration that is your soul's essence and most magnificent expression of your being.

This is not something you need to seek or strive for. Your essential nature is who you are and when all of your conditioning and programming dissolves, what remains is the truth of you—the knowing of your Higher Self.

It's easy to get derailed, to forget, to get pulled out of the heart and into the illusion of separation.

May these pages remind you of the light that emanates from your very being. May you know, without a doubt, that you are a unique extension of Creation itself.

How to Use This Book

You may use this book in any way that you feel called, of course. My intention is that you'll use it as a touchstone. A way to connect to your true nature as often as you like. These words are activations and portals into awakening your whole sovereign Self, so that you may become liberated from any limiting beliefs about you and your reality.

Start by taking a few slow, calming breaths and center your awareness in your heart. Ask Spirit, Creator, Source, God, The Great Mystery, or Love (whatever term resonates with you) what guidance will serve you today. You might ask, "Hey Source ... what would you have me know in this moment?", or "What does my Higher Self have to say about this situation or challenge?", or "What do I need to hear in this moment to be in alignment with the part of me that knows I'm whole?"

And then open the book to any page.

Read your message.

Notice how you feel in your body while reading it. Know that it doesn't have to make sense right away. Let the words into your whole being—allow the message into your life experience on every level; physically, mentally, emotionally and vibrationally.

These messages are intended to support you to live from an open heart and infinite being-ness. Ultimately these messages are from your most loving Self to you.

Why 108 Messages?

108 has been a sacred number for thousands of years. This auspicious number connects the physical realm to the metaphysical realm.

For 12 years I recited my personal mantra at least two times a day, using a traditional mala with 108 beads. This mantra was given to me by my first guru and I hold it secret and sacred. This daily practice awakened deeper focus and faith within me.

The frequency of the number 108 represents the wholeness of existence and is utilized in many traditions for prayer, prostrations, numerological calculations, ceremony, and sacred communion with the Divine.

Daily Invocation and Intention

Creator of All That Is;

I invite you into my body, mind, and heart today and everyday.

I thank you for your infinite love and energy.

May I have the clarity of mind and heart to recognize your magnificence and receive you into my life.

May I release all limiting beliefs and perceptions that no longer serve me on this journey, so that I can exist in the knowing of my Divinity, strength, perfection, and love.

May I know you through all I do, feel, and say.

May I be a vessel for your light, joy, and peace.

Thank you. Thank you. Thank you.

108 Messages

1.

You are enough.

You have always been and will always be enough.

Feel this and live from this knowing and you'll experience heaven on earth.

2.

Everything that has happened in your life
has brought you to this very moment.

There have been no mistakes.

Everything is supporting your evolution and journey
towards knowing yourself
as loved and whole.

3.

Slow down.

Slow it all down—your breath, your pace, your rushing towards ... *what*?

There's nowhere to go and nothing you need to prove.

Your existence is enough.

You are loved.

4.

You are a powerful soul—
greater than any life circumstance you'll ever endure.

5.

You are unique.

Only you can bring the medicine
of your energetic signature
to the planet.

Show up fully and authentically.
That's how you'll heal yourself and the world.

6.

Live the dream that's in your heart.

7.

Pause.
Take in a deep, slow inhalation.
Relax your jaw and shoulders.

Allow ease into your world today and remember,
your worth doesn't depend on being good,
your accomplishments,
or others liking you.

You are loved unconditionally by the very Source of Creation.

8.

What is meant for you cannot pass you by.

9.

Allow yourself to move out of your head and into your heart.
This is where your intuition lives and clear guidance resides.
Your true knowing may not be logical or even practical.
Your true knowing doesn't resemble your past.
Your true knowing may be confronting or wildly exciting.

Trust it.

10.

Doubting yourself will drain your life force.
Follow the inner impulses of what feels light and fun.
This is the path to clarity and joy.

11.

Focus on beauty.
Focus on what ignites your heart.
Focus on possibility.
Focus on the now.
Focus on gratitude.
Focus on the miracles that surround you.

12.

If you wait for ideal conditions, life will pass you by.

13.

Resentment, fear, and self-doubt
will erode you from the inside out.

Forgive yourself as a way to honor your life force,
your growth, and the energy of Source,
who loves you unconditionally.

Speak kindly to yourself.
Say loving things to your own heart.

Make your inner narrative the most beautiful love story.
Choose love of Self.

14.

Move your focus inwards—and stay in the world.
Walk with intent—and stay in the world.
Shift your attention to the magnificent—
and stay in the world.
Wake up to reality—and stay in the world.
Attune your vibration to love—and stay in the world.

15.

Every time you go against the natural flow
of your own rhythm
you corrode your inner knowing
and trust in yourself.
Your soul doesn't need to be controlled
or disciplined.
Your soul is wild and expansive,
here to remind you of the miracle that is you—
that is this life.

16.

You *are* abundance.
Practice gratitude
and you will feel this truth.

Appreciate creating this vibration internally
and you will know yourself
as the infinite nature of life itself.

This is you *being* abundance
and recognizing it's something inside of you.

17.

Have you forgotten that the miraculous exists
(and is in fact all there is)?

Go to Nature.

She'll whisper the wisdom of lifetimes
into your heart
and simultaneously leave you feeling both insignificant
and connected to the very essence
of All That Is.

Put your feet on the earth
and receive Her life force into your body.

Turn your face to the sun
and bask in the presence of this life giving consciousness.

Go to Nature and allow healing to happen.

18.

It's time to release what is no longer serving you.

Know that you are held and protected
by the love of Source.

Be gentle with yourself and continue to align
with your greatest vision for your life.

19.

Don't allow external conditions to determine
your level of joy and appreciation.

Whenever you allow someone or something
on the outside to determine your happiness,
you'll become victim to the ever changing nature of reality.

Cultivate the most loving relationship with yourself,
and Source,
because this is who you live with,
regardless of the comings and goings of life.

Creating a loving inner narrative is the path of Self mastery.

20.

There's nowhere to go.
It's all right here.
You are the answer you're seeking.
Be still and listen with your magnificent heart.

21.

Where there's scarcity, *there is no flow.*
Where there's no flow, *there is stagnation.*
Where there's stagnation, *there is disease.*

When you vibrate at a low frequency,
you prime yourself for dis-ease because
you're out of alignment with Nature.

Nature is abundant and bountiful.
It's resourceful and creative.

Just. Like. You.

22.

You'll never know
what happens next,
so soften into the mystery.
Freedom lies in the present moment.

23.

Love is your ultimate power.
Take a moment to send the vibration of love
to all who are suffering.

24.

Keep on going.

With every obstacle;
Pause.
Breathe.
Reassess.

Choose the path most aligned
with your heart and your body's YES!

25.

Experiencing fear is not the problem.
Living a fear based life is.

26.

There's nothing more natural on this planet
than you being in your essence.
Connect daily to the places, people, and experiences
that make you feel most alive.
Connect to your Self.
Practice this and your life
will be an unfolding expression
of vibrancy and joy.

27.

Keep expanding what you believe is possible.
Spirit created this entire Universe!
Believe beyond what's reasonable ...

28.

You are a limitless cosmic being.
Shine on.

29.

If you feel powerless, you're not living in your truth.

30.

The dream is within you,
and you're equipped with the capacity
to actualize it.

31.

Life has prepared you for this very moment.
This is what you came for.
Lean in.
Rise up.
Come together.
Speak truth into the light.
Gather.
Amplify your heart medicine.
Face the shadow.
Unite.
Weave magic into every breath,
like your life depends on it.

32.

Great power lies in embracing the unknown.

33.

Trust that life is supporting you.
Trust that the same energy that brought you here
will carry and champion you through every day of your life.

Trust that even when life feels terrible,
things feel hard, or you're confused;
that this too shall pass.

Trust that love permeates everything.
Trust that you're bigger than any obstacle.
Trust that every life experience is here to guide you back to
your magnificence.

Trust that you chose to be here.
Trust that there is nothing that you can't overcome.

Trust that life is magical.
Trust that what IS, is in Divine order.

34.

Get intimate
with the untamed essence
of your inner being.

35.

There's a magnificent energy that governs all of life.
Stay connected to this and you will know peace.

36.

Create your life on your terms.

37.

What if heartbreak
is a portal
to the greatest
awakening
of your life?

38.

Run from those who say they speak the truth—
> for the truth cannot be spoken.

39.

If you're operating from your old story and identity,
your reality will remain the same.

If you want a different experience of yourself and your life,
you must perceive yourself differently and tell a new story.

40.

There's nothing lacking in you.
When life feels hard;
keep loving,
keep shining,
keep saying yes to possibility.

41.

Focus less on what you think needs to be fixed or healed and more on who you came here to be.

42.

Are you making excuses
as to why you can't live the life you want
and be who you came here to be?

There's no time to waste.

The things you desire are not frivolous.

Your heart is calling you forth into your magnificence.

Follow this impulse.
Follow this knowing.

And don't look back.

43.

Rehearse the energetic imprint that you want to step into.

Spend more time focusing on who you want to be,
not who you've been.

44.

Laugh everyday!
Your laughter is medicine—for yourself and for others.

45.

During dark times—root into the unknown.
Soften into the eternal nature of your being.
Remember your breath.
Yield into the support of the earth and cosmos.

This life is but a fleeting moment
within the eternity of your unfolding.

46.

You get to choose the meaning that you associate with people, experiences, loss, and challenges. Your perception is a choice.

47.

It's a radical act to live joyfully!

48.

Time is the most precious commodity.
You won't get it back.
Choose wisely.
Honor deeply.
Love fully.

49.

Find the people who are willing to stick by you
when things get tough.
The ones who remind you of your brilliance
when the light feels dim.
And the ones who will go to wild places with you.

50.

If you're not getting what you want,
it's not because you're not deserving,
but because you're here to expand beyond your past.

Your yearning—your asking,
is coming from a limited understanding of the magnitude of who you are.
Your request is too small ... ask from your expansive soul.

51.

Until you express in the way Divinity expresses,
there will be suffering.

Until you act the way Divinity would act,
there will be suffering.

Until you think the way Divinity does,
there will be suffering.

Until you feel what Divinity feels,
there will be suffering.

Until you see yourself through the eyes of Divinity,
there will be suffering.

52.

To manifest your heart's calling,
you must embody your vision.

53.

You're a unique vibration,
a special emanation of the presence of Source.
You cannot be duplicated.
You being YOU is what matters most.
You being YOU means you're connected to Source
and that you trust in your purpose and place in this world.

54.

It's time to stop betraying yourself.
Honor your sacred yes and your sacred no.
Make yourself your priority.

55.

If you believed you were whole and complete right now,
what would you choose?

Life wants you to know yourself as whole and loved.

Make choices from this vibration—
from believing you're worthy, deserving and always supported.

56.

Trust yourself. You really do know.
Release seeking recognition, acceptance, or acknowledgement outside of yourself.
This only leads to suffering.
Cultivate your sense of Self through your relationship with Source
and feel the love that flows through you.

57.

If you want to live in a healthy body:
treat it as the sanctuary where your soul resides.
Acknowledge its strengths, beauty and power
and this will improve your energy, vitality and happiness!

58.

The world needs your light.
Don't dampen your spirit.

59.

Nature doesn't judge or discriminate.
She treats all with the same wrath
and the same compassion.
She has a way of unraveling the messiness of being human
and teaches us that duality,
when understood,
is the portal to freedom.

60.

Expedite your growth.
Get uncomfortable.

61.

You no longer need to apologize for being you.
Your presence is a gift.
Not everyone will be able to receive the gift of you—that's ok.
Only you know your motivations, your intentions,
and the grandness of your heart.

What matters most is how you feel about yourself.

62.

You are constantly awakening.
As your heart softens
and space is created
for consciousness to move through your energy field,
all that has been dormant is illuminated—
it's all been waiting patiently,
hoping that you'll recognize
the truth of your soul's essence.

63.

Every thought you think,
every feeling you have,
every word you utter,
carries a frequency.

These vibrations affect your body
and perception of reality.

The fastest way to heal
is to choose the frequency you wish to carry
and then line up your
thoughts,
words,
beliefs,
actions
and perceptions
to that.

64.

Be your truth.
Live your truth.
Love your truth.

65.

When you realize you're responsible for your own happiness, you will be free.

66.

Life is constantly changing.
Stay open when you want to shut down.
Stay curious when you feel frustrated.
Stay connected to the Source of All
and you will know peace
even in the most trying of situations.

67.

Acts of love heal all.

68.

Question everything, even your current belief system.
This is how you grow.

69.

You are not broken.
Release the illusion
that there's something wrong with you
and you'll start getting your life force back.

70.

Make a different choice today,
one that's aligned with who you're becoming.

71.

Trust your inner knowing implicitly.
Keep loving yourself and all will come to you.
Life wants you to know yourself as love.

72.

I love you.

73.

Your perception creates your reality.

You don't necessarily choose what happens in life, but you have authorship over how you respond to everyone and everything.

Your perception is yours to choose.

74.

Release clinging to what you think brings you happiness,
security, and love.

Fall in love with your relationship to Source—
with the energy that created you and All That Is.

This is where your safety lies—
in trusting that you always have everything you need
and that you're loved
and supported unconditionally by life itself.

75.

Practice getting comfortable
with letting what needs to go, go—
and letting what needs to come, come,
no matter what your opinion is about these things.

Let life show you what's best for you.

76.

Your journey may seem ludicrous or unexpected,
but it's intertwined with your soul's longing to be free.
Embrace the path that is aligned with your heart.
It will lead you through the fire,
bring you to your knees,
and show you exactly how to rise, rise, rise
and experience yourself through the eyes of love.

77.

Allow your heart to be your inner guidance system.

78.

What if grief and loss are portals
for you to discover what matters most
and to remember how delicate this life is?

79.

Look at where you spend your time, energy,
and resources—this shows what you truly value.

If there's an incongruence with how you're living and what
you're prioritizing from how you want to be living,
now's the time to course correct.

80.

Remember how magnificent you are ...

Come home to your Divinity—you were born wild and free.

Live from this space and cast your dreams into the infinite field of potentiality.

81.

The quality of attention and awareness you bring to your life greatly influences your level of contentment, happiness and bliss.

It's not what you do but *how* you do it ...

82.

You are life.
You are creating a vibrational imprint
that will transcend your existence here.
It matters.
You matter.
What you think-feel-be, matters.
More than you'll ever know.
You. Are. Loved.

83.

Let the words you choose be a blessing to others.

84.

It's not about loving yourself more,
it's about *being* yourself more.
You are already love.
Honoring who you came here to be
is the greatest expression of self-love.

85.

You are a microcosm of the macrocosm.
The entire cosmos lives inside your heart.
You are vast and miraculous.
It's time to claim who you came here to be.

86.

It takes a lot to stay open.
After all the pain and suffering ...
It takes courage to keep opening to life and love.

But please don't stop opening.
Keep showing up, even if others don't.

Keep showing up because you believe in love and in goodness
and in the pulse of breath;
and the beauty of it all.

Keep giving life everything you've got.
It's here that you'll meet yourself.

87.

Don't waste any more time!
Make that phone call, express how you really feel,
quit the job, take the job,
love your own tender heart,
go beyond the known, say yes to yourself,
do something different, stop pleasing everyone but yourself,
know you're worth it, set a boundary, give yourself permission,
let go ...
Say yes to the mystery of it all.
You are being carried.

88.

Remember to laugh.
Your laughter will heal your body, your heart and your mind.
It's the most potent form of medicine there is.

89.

You were made for these times.
You were made completely whole and capable
of navigating all your life experiences.
There's no mistaking what you've been through,
what you've accomplished,
and what you will grow into in this life.
Remember: you were made for these times.

90.

If you knew
without a shadow of doubt
that better things would come ...
would you let go of what you're clinging to?

91.

Get to know your shadow.
Give yourself permission to feel it,
be with it, and even honor it.
Your inner light will automatically expand as an
acknowledgement of you returning to your wholeness.

92.

Love wants to touch you,
move through you,
animate your very existence.
Make space for love.

93.

Time is your most valuable commodity;
you don't get it back.
Choose what you do, who you do it with,
and how you *be*, very wisely.
This day matters.

94.

You can heal yourself
by placing your awareness
on what you're genuinely feeling grateful for.
Allow gratitude to fill your whole body,
mind, and heart space.

95.

Life will not unfold the way you want it to all of the time
(have you noticed?).

Your authorship is how you *be* with yourself
through the not-liking-what's-happening parts.

Instead of fighting with reality
and using your energy to resist what is,
focus your attention inwards to stay present with yourself
through the discomfort.

No longer will you abandon your own tender heart.
No longer will you wait for the external world to change
in order for you to be ok.

Cultivate your inner strength
through loving thoughts to your Self.
Self compassion is the balm for your tender heart.

96.

Set yourself free from people who do not honor and respect you.
This includes the version of you that does not honor and respect you.

97.

Your present is not defined by your past.
You were a soul long before you were a human in this body.
Life will offer you the grandest experiences
to break your heart open
to love some more—in order to remember your wholeness.
A Divine plan is unfolding as your life right now.

98.

You are not your past.
Keep choosing who you are being ...
moment to moment, breath by breath.

99.

Offer up any pain and suffering to the Divine.
Release the burden of being addicted to believing you're not worthy.
There couldn't be anything further from the truth.
Know this, feel this, and live this - and you will be free.

100.

What if your perceived challenges
don't have to be so significant?

What if they don't have to take up so much space
in your mind, heart, and being?

Your perspective is your choice.

When you understand this,
you're able to choose where to place your
focus, attention, and energy.

This, my dear, is ultimate freedom.

101.

Lean into the great mystery of life.
Say yes to the magic and magnificence that is here now.

102.

Adversity is here to accelerate your evolution.

103.

This day matters and you matter.

Your life force is intrinsic to the fabric of this reality.

If you were not here, the entire world would be altered …

And once you are gone, it will be forever changed.

104.

Your spirit has the power to awaken others.

Don't underestimate the impact of your presence.

105.

Dance. Just dance.
Right here, right now.
There's no need for it to be good or pretty or right.
Allow your body to move in any way it wants.
Let your Spirit soar.

106.

Wholeness is your most natural state of being. Experiencing wholeness is the alchemy for true healing to occur.

107.

People and experiences are catalysts
for your unhealed patterns to become visible
so you can heal
by recalibrating to the frequency
of wholeness and love.

108.

Nothing can diminish the eternal light that is your soul.
You're more powerful than you have yet realized.

About the Author

Melanie (Madhuri) Phillips

As a dedicated Evolution Coach and Spiritual Mentor, Melanie is renowned for her ability to lead individuals towards their authentic essence and untapped potential.

Certified as a Clinical Ayurvedic Specialist, Yoga Teacher Trainer, and Energy Healer, Melanie's journey has been one of resolute healing, navigating through the realms of chronic illness and profound loss. She ardently champions the belief that every individual possesses the power to emerge from shadows, rediscovering their inherent light.

An accomplished author, Melanie is the visionary behind the bestselling book "Living After Loss: A Soulful Guide to Freedom," delving into the depths of resilience and renewal. Additionally, she co-authored the influential work "Your Irresistible Life: 4 Seasons of Self-Care through Ayurveda & Yoga Practices that Work," which has resonated with countless seekers on their wellness journey.

As the host of the inspirational "Be The Light Podcast," Melanie skillfully intertwines her personal transformative journey with illuminating dialogues featuring diverse guests, collectively empowering listeners to courageously embrace their inner light and embark on a profound voyage of self-discovery.

Melanie guides clients worldwide through her transformative online mentorship programs and retreats—supporting them to uncover and release the root cause of imbalance which results in creating a life in alignment with their highest potential.

madhurimethod.com

Manufactured by Amazon.ca
Bolton, ON